DUMB CANE

AND

DAFFODILS

POISONOUS PLANTS

IN THE

HOUSE AND GARDEN

CAROL LERNER

Morrow Junior Books · New York

The author thanks Floyd Swink, Taxonomist of the Morton Arboretum in Lisle, Illinois, for his review of the manuscript.

Printed in Hong Kong by South China Printing Company (1988) Ltd.
1 2 3 4 5 6 7 8 9 10
Library of Congress Cataloging-in-Publication Data
Lerner, Carol.
Dumb cane and daffodils : poisonous plants in the house and garden
/ Carol Lerner.
p. cm.
Includes index.
Summary: Describes the physical characteristics, natural habitats,
and harmful effects of several varieties of plants grown in North
America.
ISBN 0-688-08791-4. —ISBN 0-688-08796-5 (lib. bdg.)
1. Poisonous plants—Juvenile literature. 2. Plants, Ornamental—
Toxicology—Juvenile literature. 3. Vegetables—Toxicology—
Juvenile literature. [1. Poisonous plants.] I. Title.
QK100.A1L47 1990
581.6'9—dc20   89-33622   CIP   AC

CONTENTS

Introduction *4*

Chapter One **Down the Garden Path** *6*

Chapter Two **Shrubs and Climbers** *17*

Chapter Three **The Vegetable Patch** *22*

Chapter Four **The Indoor Garden** *25*

Index *32*

Introduction

Any family with small children in the house tries to keep them from danger. Medicines, matches, and cleaning chemicals are stored out of reach because the very young may put anything in their mouths. But few people realize that the plants which decorate their house or yard could be just as dangerous.

Most ornamental plants in and around our homes were brought from other parts of the world, but many now grow from coast to coast in North America. Quite a few have spread into areas where no one ever planted them. Like many native American plants, some of these imported ones contain poisons. A number of these poisonous species are common plants around our homes and yards.

Children under the age of five are the most frequent victims of plant poisoning, and they are likely to suffer most severely because of their smaller body weight. In older children and adults, the poison becomes more diluted as it moves through their larger bodies. But teens and adults, too, may suffer from poisoning after an experiment with an unknown plant—from eating some part or from brewing teas with leaves or flowers. Sometimes household animals also chew on plants.

Of course, not all poisonous plants and not all poisons are equally dangerous. Some cause mild discomfort, while others can kill. The same plant may not be equally dangerous in all circumstances. Its poisons may be powerful only at certain stages of the plant's growth. Or a plant growing in one place may contain more poison than the same species in another location.

There are more complicating factors. While some dangerous species have poison throughout the plant body, others have some parts that are harmless. The poison may be carried only in the leaves, the fruits, or the underground parts. In any case, not everyone reacts to a poison in the same way, because some people are more sensitive than others. Animals also have different responses: A cat may get sick from a plant that a rabbit can eat without harm.

Some closely related plants share the same poison, and a few plant families contain an unusually large number of poisonous species. But a great many families among the flowering plants have some poisonous members, and it is really impossible to recognize a plant as dangerous without knowing its particular species. Garden catalogs are not reliable guides: They give warnings about some species but not about all of them. At best, a houseplant from the florist has a tag indicating its name and giving some advice about plant care, but no notice of the poison it may contain.

A very small number of plants are such a great threat that they should not be grown where young children live. However, most plants that contain poison can still be enjoyed around the home if they are handled sensibly. Obviously they must be kept away from a child who cannot understand the danger. Older children (and adults!) can learn not to taste, eat, swallow, or chew on any part of any plant unless they know with certainty what it is and that it is harmless.

Since poisons may remain even after a plant is dead and dry, clippings or fruits of poisonous species growing outdoors should be taken from the yard and disposed of safely. Inside the house, leaves, flowers, and fruits of houseplants that drop to the floor should be picked up as soon as they fall. Care should be taken with containers of cut flowers, too, since some plants poison the water they stand in.

Every member of the household should know the phone number and location of the nearest poison control center. If someone eats part of a plant and is in pain, he or she needs to be brought to a doctor quickly. If you know which plant was eaten but don't know its name, take a sample along with the patient.

The plants included here are only a selection from the many that may be hazardous. I chose those that have some history of causing human poisonings and are grown over wide areas of North America. Many poisonous plants that thrive only in the warmest parts of the United States (Florida and the far Southwest) were omitted. If you want to know more about some particular plant, most libraries have reference books about poisonous plants which you can consult. A few books are listed on page 31.

The names of the plants shown in the colored illustrations appear in capital letters when they are first discussed. All plants are called by their most common name (or names) in the chapters. Latin, or scientific, names are given in the index.

Chapter One
DOWN THE GARDEN PATH

As soon as the ice of winter melts from the ground, the first spring plants push their leaves up from the warming earth. These early plants grow quickly and rush into bloom on the first mild days. The SNOW-DROP, with two grass-like leaves and a single hanging flower, may blossom while snow is still on the ground.

Plants in the genus NARCISSUS are probably the most familiar blossoms of early spring and include daffodils and jonquils. They all have flowers of yellow or white, with an outer collar and a cup-like center. HYACINTH (HIGH-ah-sinth) has crowded clusters of pink, blue, or white flowers.

Most of the earliest flowers owe their quick start to a supply of food that has been stored over the winter in underground bulbs. Any time we eat an onion, we are feeding on the food energy in a plant bulb. Along with this supply of nourishment, however, the bulbs of some common spring garden plants also contain a store of poisons.

In Holland during World War Two, food for farm animals was in short supply, and some of them were in danger of starving. Since Holland raises flower bulbs to sell all over the world, there were plenty of these on hand. The Dutch farmers began feeding their animals bulbs of snowdrops, narcissus, and hyacinths, hoping the livestock would be able to digest this unusual food. Instead, the animals became sick.

But we rarely feed people from our flower garden, and you may wonder how a human being would be likely to eat bulbs. It is not so

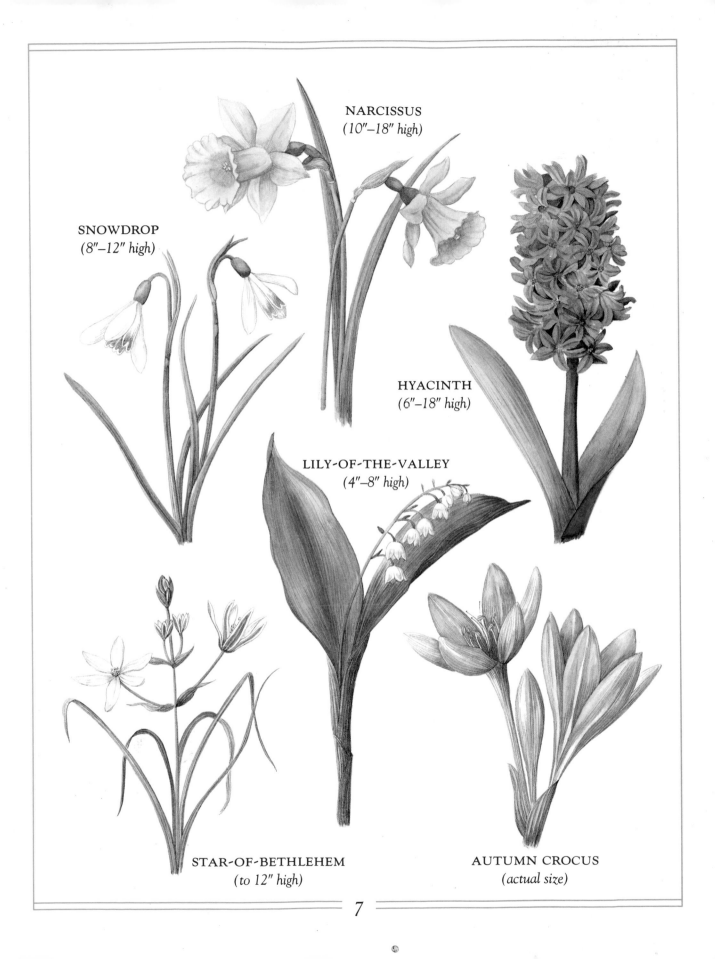

NARCISSUS
(10″–18″ high)

SNOWDROP
(8″–12″ high)

HYACINTH
(6″–18″ high)

LILY-OF-THE-VALLEY
(4″–8″ high)

STAR-OF-BETHLEHEM
(to 12″ high)

AUTUMN CROCUS
(actual size)

NARCISSUS BULB

hard to imagine how this has happened. Bulbs are often kept in the house or basement before planting. If they are stored without identification, any one of them might be mistaken for some kind of onion and eaten by a young child or used in preparing food. Bulbs of narcissus are the easiest to confuse with onions, and they can cause death if they are eaten in large amounts.

STAR-OF-BETHLEHEM is another common spring flower with a poisonous bulb. Its leaves and flowers can also be dangerous. The plant is easy to recognize by the green stripe on the back of each petal. Star-of-Bethlehem sometimes escapes from the garden and takes root on roadsides and in fields. Because freezing or plowing of the ground pushes the bulbs to the surface, many sheep and cattle have died from eating them in pastures. Children have become sick after eating the flowers or bulbs.

LILY-OF-THE-VALLEY
BERRIES
(actual size)

Everyone knows LILY-OF-THE-VALLEY. The small white bell-shaped flowers hang in one-sided clusters and fill the air with perfume in late spring. Although all parts of the plant are dangerous, most poisonings are the result of eating the bright red berries. These ripen in the summer and are attractive to children. When lily-of-the-valley is picked and brought inside, the water in which the flowers are kept also becomes poisonous.

The spring crocus blooms early, with narrow grass-like leaves and flowers in all shades of yellow, purple, and white. Each flower has six petal-like parts that join in a thin tube. Other species of crocus, similar in appearance, flower in the fall. Crocuses are not poisonous.

The plant called AUTUMN CROCUS, or meadow saffron, has purple or white flowers similar to those of the

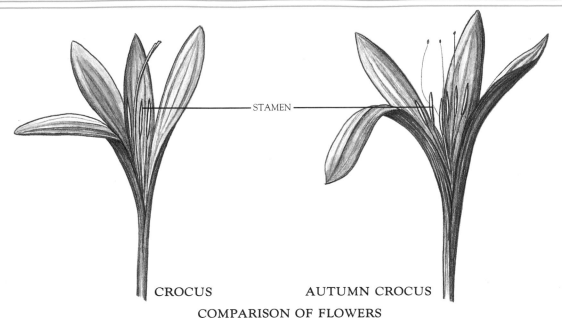

CROCUS   AUTUMN CROCUS

COMPARISON OF FLOWERS

(two of the outer flower segments were removed from each)

crocus; but it is an entirely different species and belongs to another plant family. Its flowers have six yellow stamens (the male parts in the middle of a flower) rather than the three stamens of a true crocus. Also unlike the crocus, the autumn crocus plant is always without leaves at the time of flowering. Its leaves come up after the blooms are finished and die off before the plant flowers again. The flowers and fat underground stems of autumn crocus contain the greatest amount of poison, but all parts can be dangerous if they are eaten.

Many popular plants of the summer flower garden carry their own load of danger. DELPHINIUM (dell-FIN-ee-um) grows as a wild plant with blue or purple flowers over much of the United States and Canada, but the garden versions are far more showy than the native wildflowers.

Garden species may be perennials (plants that come up again year after year) or annuals (plants that live for a single year). Even though these plants all belong to the genus *Delphinium*, gardeners usually refer to the perennials as delphiniums and to the annuals as larkspurs. These garden flowers are most often blue or purple but also come in white and pink. They bloom in a mass, crowded on top of tall, dramatic spikes.

DELPHINIUM
SEED
(enlarged)

Young delphinium and larkspur plants are highly dangerous, but the amount of poison in the leaves and stems decreases as they age. All parts of the mature plant remain poisonous, but by the time the plant makes seeds, the poison in the leaves is down to a small fraction of what it was. Now the seeds are the most dangerous part. Earlier in this century, these seeds were ground up and sold in powders to kill head and body lice, but today it is thought to be unhealthy to use this poison on the body.

FOUR-O'CLOCK is an old-fashioned garden favorite that is usually grown as an annual from seeds. Coming from the West Indies and tropical parts of the Americas, it is sometimes called the marvel-of-Peru. The sweet-smelling flowers—white, yellow, red, or pink—open in late afternoon. They close under the full sun of the next morning, each flower lasting only one day. Children like to chew on the ribbed seeds. Both roots and seeds of four-o'clock contain a poison that can cause severe stomach upset and pain.

FOUR-O'CLOCK ROOT AND SEED
(actual size)   *(enlarged)*

Often the poisonous parts of a plant will also cause skin rashes when they are handled. As with poison ivy, not everyone is sensitive to the touch of these plants. But four-o'clock seeds and roots, for example, may irritate the skin, and some people get "lily rash" from handling narcissus or hyacinth bulbs or plants.

One group of plants that is often used in gardens—and also indoors as houseplants—can cause very severe blistering and a rash. These plants are called spurges and belong to the genus *Euphorbia* (you-FOR-bee-ah). The milky white sap in the stems and leaves of most *Euphorbia* plants is extremely irritating.

DELPHINIUM
(1′–5′ high)

FOUR-O'CLOCK
(1′–3′ high)

SNOW-ON-THE-MOUNTAIN
(to 2′ high)

CASTOR BEAN
(3′–15′ high)

A number of *Euphorbia* species are sold through garden catalogs for outdoor use. The most popular of these is SNOW-ON-THE-MOUNTAIN, which is planted because of its decorative white-edged leaves rather than for its tiny flowers. Snow-on-the-mountain is a native plant in the North American West and grows in the wild from Canada to Mexico. It is planted in gardens from coast to coast.

The thick milky juice of this plant is so powerful that it has been used in place of a hot branding iron to mark the hides of cattle in Texas. The sap causes severe pain when it touches the eyes, mouth, nostrils, or an open cut on the skin. Snow-on-the-mountain and other spurges have poisoned people who ate parts of the plants and have even caused some deaths.

OPIUM POPPY

A few garden plants have been singled out by law, making it a crime to grow them. The poppy species that is the source of the opium drug was once a common garden plant, but now its cultivation is illegal. Several other types of poppies are planted in gardens, including the oriental poppy, Iceland poppy, and celandine, or rock, poppy. Although none of these is on record as having caused human poisoning in North America, all of them contain some poison.

The CASTOR BEAN plant is another outlaw, though it is illegal only in some California counties. This strange plant comes from Africa and grows best in warm climates. Starting from a seed, it may shoot up ten or twelve feet or more in a single summer. Castor oil—once used as a medicine but now mainly as a machine oil—comes from its seeds. In some southern states, castor beans are grown commercially for this oil. Because of their rapid growth and large, handsome leaves, they are also used in gardens. In the North, it is not unusual to

CASTOR BEAN
FRUIT AND SEEDS
(actual size)

see them planted in public parks.

It is safe to swallow castor oil because the poisons are left behind when the oil is squeezed from the seeds to make the medicine. But the shiny black-and-brown seeds themselves are deadly. Unlike castor oil, the seeds have a pleasant taste and so are tempting to children. Even one or two of them can be fatal, and they have caused many poisonings. If the castor bean is grown in gardens, the flower stalks can be removed as soon as they appear to prevent seeds from developing. However, the leaves and other parts of the plant also contain some poison.

Four other plants with deadly poisons are very commonly sold by garden supply houses. Since all four have been used in medicines, their power to affect the human body for good or ill is well known. Drugs from plants—used in amounts that are carefully measured—can overcome the effects of certain human diseases. But anyone who eats the plant is swallowing a dose of unknown strength and may be poisoned.

The European FOXGLOVE only came into medical use about two hundred years ago, but it already had a place in folk medicine. Although drugs made from foxglove have proved to be extremely valuable in treating some kinds of heart disease, the chemicals in this plant may also cause heart failure.

Purple foxglove has hanging bell-like flowers, spotted on the inside, growing on a tall stem. It comes in shades of pink and white as well as purple. All parts contain a slightly sweet-tasting poison that can cause death. Children have become ill from sucking the flowers and from eating leaves or seeds. Water in a vase holding foxglove flowers becomes poisonous.

BLACK HENBANE was being used in herbal medicines to dull the pain of toothache over three thousand years ago. In modern times, a

It is easy to see why CHRISTMAS ROSE, or black hellebore (HELL-ah-bore), attracts gardeners. If the plant is protected from the most severe cold, its large white flowers will open in the dead of winter. Hellebore, too, is an ancient poison that was supposedly used in witches' charms. Any part of the plant can cause vomiting and convulsions, and may lead to death by interfering with normal breathing. Until the eighteenth century, it was also given to cure people of worms in the intestine. A magazine from that time remarks that the drug will surely get rid of the worms, but warns that it may also take the life of the patient!

Chapter Two
SHRUBS AND CLIMBERS

Some of our most familiar bushes and vines—plants found on almost any city block—have histories that include cases of human poisoning. Usually the fruits are the cause of the trouble. They look enough like familiar foods to tempt someone to take a taste.

PRIVET FLOWERS
(actual size)

Privet (it rhymes with "rivet") is probably the single most common bush planted around homes in the United States and Canada, and it has been with us for a long time. The COMMON PRIVET was brought from Europe in early colonial times, and Asian species were introduced in the nineteenth century. Privet is popular because it grows quickly, even in poor soil and under difficult conditions. In fact, once these shrubs have taken hold, it is almost impossible to kill them.

Privet has shiny leaves that grow in opposite pairs along the stem. Clusters of small white flowers bloom in early summer at the tips of its branches. Blue-black berries ripen in the fall and stay on the twigs all through the winter. Birds usually ignore the bitter berries, but occasionally they do eat some of them. They drop the seeds after eating the fruit, spreading privet bushes into forests and open fields. The birds seem to be unaffected by the poison that is contained in the berries—and in all parts of the plant—but children have suffered illness and even death from eating privet berries.

YEW is another popular choice for hedges in yards and gardens. Two kinds of yew are native to the woods of North America, but the ones planted around houses are usually species that came from England or Japan. Dark evergreen needles make yew a beautiful plant in all seasons of the year.

YEW FRUIT WITH
SEED, CUT OPEN
(enlarged)

The flat needles grow in two opposite rows along the stem and come to a sharp point at the tips. Male and female flowers grow on separate plants. The female plants are easy to recognize by their berry-like fruits of coral red. Each fruit is shaped like a little cup, open at the top, holding a single large brown or greenish seed.

In Europe, the yew was another of the plants that was believed to have gone into witches' brews, and it was used as a symbol of death. It was said that people could die after merely resting in the shade of a yew tree. This is not true, although there is a strong poison in the leaves, seeds, and bark that can be deadly if it is eaten. Along with other effects, the poison slows the heart and makes it hard to breathe. The bright attractive fruits are tempting, especially to children. In view of their poisonous seeds, it is a good idea to pick off the fruits of yew plants growing around homes where very young children live.

The COMMON HYDRANGEA (high-DRAIN-juh), like the privet, is popular because it grows quickly and needs little care. This is a bold plant, and everything about it is big—the clusters of flowers and the bush itself, which may grow to twenty or thirty feet. The flowers bloom late in the summer, much later than other shrubs and trees. Most of the flowers make no fruits but remain on the bush and dry slowly, changing in color from white to pink to brown. Other kinds of garden hydrangeas have pink or blue blossoms.

The leaves and buds of this bush are poisonous. The best-known case of poisoning occurred when a Florida family added flower buds from their Japanese hydrangea to a mixed salad. All kinds of hydrangeas, both native and garden species, are believed to contain poison.

COMMON PRIVET
(leaf 1″–2½″)

COMMON HYDRANGEA
(flower cluster 6″–12″)

YEW
(needle ¾″–1¼″)

WISTERIA
(flower cluster 6″–12″)

DAPHNE
(leaf 2″–3″)

ENGLISH IVY
(leaf ½″–5″)

The DAPHNE (DAFF-nee) bush has been known to be dangerous ever since ancient times. Merely rubbing its leaves against the skin will cause blisters. In past centuries, when it was still common practice to apply leeches to draw blood from sick people in an attempt to cure them, daphne bark was used in a similar way: A patch of bark placed against the skin caused blistering and was thought to remove the illness. Eating any part of daphne is irritating and causes swelling, burning, and bleeding in the whole digestive system. Just ten fruits—each one about the size of a pea—may be enough to kill a child.

The most commonly planted species of daphne has clusters of rosy-purple flowers that bloom on bare stems in early spring. The leaves reach their full size only after the flowers have bloomed. The dangerous fruits—bright red and shiny—ripen in August and September.

ENGLISH IVY
FRUITS
(*slightly enlarged*)

ENGLISH IVY is another European species that has been recognized as poisonous for centuries. Like so many other plants containing poison, ivy had a place in many folk remedies. Among other things, the leaf was used to cure the pain of toothache and corns, to treat wounds, and to get rid of fleas.

These ivy plants are easy to grow and are very often used as a ground cover in shady yards. There are dozens of kinds of English ivy, differing from each other in leaf shape and color. Some of the more decorative ones are also used as potted houseplants.

English ivy has tough, evergreen leaves. In outline, a typical leaf has three to five rounded points, like a small maple leaf. The plant sends out little roots all along the stem. These rootlets cling to any rough surface and permit the plant to grow on walls, tree trunks, and fences. The plant produces flowers only if it grows in a sunny place. The flowers are small and green and easy to overlook. The fruit is a cluster of black berries, each with several seeds. Children have been poisoned by eating these bitter berries. Some people are allergic to the leaves and get skin rashes from touching them.

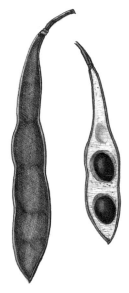

WISTERIA PODS
RIGHT: CUT OPEN,
SHOWING SEEDS
(½ actual size)

WISTERIA (wis-TEER-ee-ah) is a very different kind of plant, with masses of showy flowers in long hanging clusters. The blossoms are blue, purple, or white. A member of the pea family, wisteria has a typical sweet-pea flower and seeds that grow in thick pods. It is often planted next to porches, where the stem of the vine climbs by twisting itself around a post or some other kind of support.

Eating any part of this handsome plant causes severe stomach pain and upset. Most poisonings occur when children nibble on the pods or seeds, for two seeds are enough to make a child sick. One scientist reports that the poison in the seeds can kill cockroaches. Fortunately the human victims usually recover in a day or two.

Chapter Three
THE VEGETABLE PATCH

We can find at least a few poisonous plants in almost every part of the vast plant kingdom—among the ferns, the mushrooms, and the many different families of flowering plants. A few plant families are notorious because they contain so many poisonous species. Among these sinister families, the nightshades are the most famous.

We met two of its members—henbane and deadly nightshade—growing in the flower garden. Two other species are everyday vegetables that contain poisons in parts of the plant that are not normally eaten. However, the home gardener may be tempted to find some use for these inedible parts.

FRUITS OF A
POTATO PLANT
(2/3 actual size)

Almost the whole potato plant, except for the potatoes themselves, can be dangerous. The potatoes are tubers, the swollen parts of an underground stem. Above ground, the leafy branches produce round green fruits that are about the size of a grape. If the potatoes grow close to the surface of the earth, or if they are left in the sun, they sometimes turn green, too. The fruits, stems, and all other green parts of the potato plant contain poison.

Illness and some deaths have resulted from eating green potatoes, and farm animals have died after being fed with uprooted potato plants or spoiled potatoes. Green spots on potatoes and any sprouts growing from the eyes should be cut out completely before cooking the food. Spoiled potatoes should be thrown away.

In the case of tomatoes, the fruit is the part of the plant that we eat. In the 1500s, New World explorers discovered tomatoes being grown as a food crop by Latin American Indians. Along with captured gold and other treasures, they carried the plant back home to Europe. But for centuries Europeans refused to eat tomatoes, recognizing the plant as a member of the nightshade family and believing it to be poisonous.

The leaves and stems of tomato plants actually do contain the same poison that is found in its close relative, the potato. Children have become sick from drinking a tea made from the leaves, and a few people find that their skin breaks out after handling the plants. Barnyard animals have died from eating the leaves and stems of tomato plants in the garden.

The pea family, which contains both beans and peas, is extremely important in feeding the world's people and their farm animals. Yet this family also includes a great number of plants that contain dangerous poisons. Some species of sweet peas, lupines, and locoweeds have poisoned livestock and (occasionally) people, as well. Rosary pea, also called crab's eye or precatory bean, contains one of the most powerful poisons of any plant. The shiny red-

ROSARY PEAS
(twice actual size)

and-black seed grows on a common tropical vine and is often brought home by tourists in a piece of costume jewelry or some other souvenir. Chewing and eating a single rosary pea can be fatal, even to an adult.

As with wisteria, a member of the pea family sometimes causes trouble simply because the fruits of an inedible plant (that is, the beans or peas in their pod) look so much like a garden vegetable that someone decides to eat them. One kind of garden bean plant can also be dangerous: The *raw* beans and pods of the scarlet runner bean contain small amounts of poison that upset the stomach and digestive system. Cooking destroys this poison.

The leaves of rhubarb plants must never be used for food. Every bit of green leaf should be cut off when the red or green stems are being prepared for cooking. The sour-tasting stems are delicious (after the addition of enough sugar). But eating rhubarb leaves may damage the kidneys and can kill.

Rhubarb resembles another vegetable plant called rhubarb chard, a variety of Swiss chard with red stems. Like all chards, both the stems and leaves are eaten. Rhubarb stalks are usually longer and thicker than the leaf stems of chard. The knowledgeable gardener is not likely to confuse the two, but an inexperienced visitor could.

ASPARAGUS BERRIES
(actual size)

Asparagus, like rhubarb, is a perennial plant—one that comes up every spring from a long-living underground rootstock. Some of the thick young shoots are cut for eating when they are just a few inches high. The shoots that are not cut grow into tall plants with many fern-like branches. Each plant is either male or female. The female plants produce bright red berries that look good enough to eat.

Some people break out in blisters and skin rashes when they eat raw asparagus spears. Eating the berries can have the same effect upon sensitive people.

No one should harvest food from the vegetable garden without being certain about what is growing there. It is equally important to recognize the edible and inedible parts of each kind of food plant.

Chapter Four
The Indoor Garden

Most houseplants are natives of the tropics. Because winter temperatures are mild in their homelands, these plants keep their leaves all through the year. The temperatures within our houses imitate the year-round warmth of the tropics and make it possible for these green plants to grow indoors when those outside are frozen and brown.

A single plant family, the arum, provides some of the commonest indoor plants—the kinds that are sold in every dime store. Arums can be recognized by their unique arrangement of flowers. These are tiny, and they grow in a cluster on a spike. The flower cluster is usually surrounded by a leaf-like hood of green or white or some other color.

But many arums that are houseplants are grown only for their shiny dark leaves and almost never flower indoors. This is true of the PHILODENDRON (fill-o-DEN-drun), probably the most common houseplant of all. It is easy to grow and needs little care. The most familiar kind is a climbing plant with a heart-shaped leaf, but there are over two hundred different species and varieties of philodendron, with leaves in many different shapes, sometimes marked with light green, white, yellow, or red.

Another arum, DUMB CANE or dieffenbachia (dee-fen-BOCK-ee-ah), is almost as popular. It has large, broad leaves that grow from a single stem, and some kinds are spattered with white markings. The name dumb cane suggests the danger in *all* plants of the arum family. Their leaves—and sometimes other plant parts as well—contain sharp crystals. If the plant is chewed or eaten, these crystals cut into the mouth and throat like hundreds of burning spears. The tongue, mouth, and throat swell, sometimes so badly that it becomes impossible to breathe.

Most poisonings from philodendron and dieffenbachia do not reach this degree of seriousness, but between them they probably poison more children than all other kinds of plants put together. Sometimes the family pet falls victim. Cats are notorious for eating household greenery, and many of them have chewed on arums. Often these cats do not survive.

Other arums—all containing the same irritating crystals—are popular for their large and beautiful leaves. The climbing plant called CUT-LEAF PHILODENDRON has an unusual leaf that looks as if it had been cut with a scissors along each side. It is seen everywhere—in lobbies, in apartments and houses, in dentists' offices.

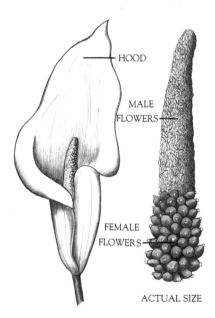

HOOD

MALE FLOWERS

FEMALE FLOWERS

ACTUAL SIZE

½ ACTUAL SIZE

ARUM FLOWERS
(calla lily)

Plants from at least three different plant groups, or genera, within the arum family are all called ELEPHANT EAR when they are sold as houseplants. They all have big, handsome, arrow-shaped leaves. The elephant-ear plants in the genus *Caladium* (cah-LAY-dee-um), also called angel wings, are the most striking. Depending upon the species and variety, caladiums have leaves of green and white, pink, or red. Unlike most tropical plants, caladium's bright leaves die down at the end of summer and the plant enters a resting period in the fall.

A smaller number of arums are sold as flowering houseplants. When flowers are present on the plants, there is no doubt about family identification. The

PHILODENDRON
(leaf 4"–15")

CUT-LEAF PHILODENDRON
(leaf 16"–36")

DUMB CANE
(leaf 10"–24")

CALLA LILY
(leaf 10"–18")

ELEPHANT EAR
(leaf 9"–30")

arum known as CALLA LILY is probably the one seen most often in flower. It, too, has shiny, arrow-shaped leaves (spotted with silver in some species). In the most common species of calla lily, the leafy hood around the flower cluster is white. These dramatic flowers also appear in arrangements of cut plants from florists and are sometimes grown outdoors.

POINSETTIA FLOWERS AT THE
CENTER OF RED BRACTS
(*actual size*)

A couple of other troublesome plant groups show up regularly on the indoor windowsill. POINSETTIA (poyn-SET-tee-ah) is a favorite Christmas gift plant. The bright red (or pink or white) "petals" at the top of its stems are actually bracts, a kind of leaf. The tiny yellow flowers bloom in the center of these bracts.

Poinsettia belongs to the genus *Euphorbia*. This is the plant group that includes snow-on-the-mountain, with milky sap that burns and blisters. Poinsettia sap, found mainly in the leaves and stems, is also irritating. In 1919, when a two-year-old in Hawaii was reported to have died after eating a poinsettia leaf, this plant got the reputation of being a killer. Since then, many more children have chewed on poinsettias in their homes and have suffered from stomach pains and irritation of the digestive system as a result. Some cases have been severe, but there have been no deaths. It seems likely that the plant does not usually contain enough poison to kill. But there is no doubt that it should be kept out of the reach of young children.

CROWN OF THORNS is another *Euphorbia* used as a houseplant. It has small leaves, and stems that are covered with sharp gray or green thorns. As in poinsettia, the flowers are tiny, but the red bracts that

POINSETTIA
(leaf 3"–6")

JERUSALEM CHERRY
(leaf 2"–4")

CROWN OF THORNS
(leaf 1"–2½")

AMARYLLIS
(1'–3' high)

OLEANDER
(leaf 4"–12")

surround them provide bright color. The milky sap of this *Euphorbia* also burns and irritates.

Because of its holiday colors, JERUSALEM CHERRY is another plant that appears in florist stores around Christmastime. It has shiny pointed leaves and small fruits that ripen to a bright red or orange. They look like cherry tomatoes. The plant is, in fact, related to the tomato and is a member of the nightshade family. There is some question about how dangerous Jerusalem cherry really is. Its leaves probably contain poison. Its green fruits certainly do, and the ripe fruits may be poisonous as well.

Some of the same bulbs that flower outdoors in early spring are also grown in the house in wintertime. Indoors, with the proper handling, they can be "forced" into bloom as early as January or February. Paperwhite narcissus is one of the easiest to force and probably the most common indoor bulb. Narcissus and other poisonous outdoor bulbs were discussed earlier. Obviously, the chance that a child may try to eat one of these flower bulbs is that much greater when the plants sit indoors on a table or window ledge.

AMARYLLIS (am-ah-RILL-lis) gives its name to the amaryllis plant family—a family that includes narcissus, daffodil, and other members with poisonous bulbs. Amaryllis bulbs are grown indoors and often bloom around the holiday season. These are truly spectacular plants, with big, bright, trumpet-shaped flowers of red, white, pink, or orange on top of tall, thick stems. Like many flower bulbs, they can be mistaken for onions—and they have been. Amaryllis bulbs cause stomachache and other digestive pains. The poison in one species is said to interfere with normal breathing.

Perhaps the most dangerous plant ever grown in the home is the beautiful OLEANDER (OH-lee-ann-der). It has bushy stems with stiff, narrow leaves. Showy flowers of pink, red, or white bloom at the ends of its branches. Oleander is grown as an indoor plant in the north and as an outdoor shrub in California, Florida, and other warm areas of the United States. Indoors or out, it is risky.

The poison in oleander acts quickly and violently, and may bring death within a day. Eating or sucking on its flowers, leaves, or stems can cause severe illness, at the very least. Food that touches the sap of this plant may become poisonous. A California child died after using a peeled oleander twig as a skewer to cook a hot dog over the campfire.

A person can be hurt by oleander even without touching the plant. Breathing the smoke of burning branches can cause poisoning, and just smelling the flowers may harm someone who has asthma or heart trouble. Certainly people who grow oleander should understand these facts and take steps to protect themselves and others from its poison.

The plants in this book—like all plants—add beauty and interest to our surroundings. A very small number of poisonous plants can present a serious threat to health in spite of the most careful handling. But aside from these few, there is no reason to remove all poisonous species from the home. We can learn to recognize those that may cause harm. And then, knowing their danger, we can handle them with appropriate care and enjoy them in safety.

For Further Reading

These books include both wild and cultivated plants.

Lampe, Kenneth F., and Mary Ann McCann. *AMA Handbook of Poisonous and Injurious Plants.* Chicago: American Medical Association, 1985.

Schmutz, Ervin M., and Lucretia B. Hamilton. *Plants That Poison.* Flagstaff: Northland Press, 1979. Emphasizes plants of the southwestern United States, but many of the species are found coast to coast.

Westbrooks, Randy G., and James W. Preacher. *Poisonous Plants of Eastern North America.* Columbia: University of South Carolina Press, 1986.

Index

The scientific names are shown in *italics*. The illustration pages appear in **boldface.**

amaryllis (*Hippeastrum*), **29**, 30
  family (*Amaryllidaceae*), 30
angel wings, *see* elephant ear
arum family (*Araceae*), 25-26, **26**
asparagus (*Asparagus officinalis*), 24, **24**
autumn crocus (*Colchicum autumnale*), **7**, 8-9, **9**
belladonna, *see* deadly nightshade
black henbane (*Hyoscyamus niger*), 13-14, **14**, **15**, 22
Caladium, *see* elephant ear
calla lily (*Zantedeschia aethiopica*), **26**, **27**, 28
castor bean (*Ricinus communis*), **11**, 12-13, **13**
Christmas rose (*Helleborus niger*), **15**, 16
common hydrangea (*Hydrangea paniculata*), 18, **19**
common privet (*Ligustrum vulgare*), 17, **17**, **19**
crab's eye, *see* rosary pea
crocus (*Crocus*), 8, 9, **9**
crown of thorns (*Euphorbia milii*), 28, **29**, 30
cut-leaf philodendron (*Monstera deliciosa*), 26, **27**
daffodil (*Narcissus*), 6
daphne (*Daphne mezereum*), **19**, 20
deadly nightshade (*Atropa belladonna*), 14, **14**, **15**, 22
delphinium (*Delphinium*), 9-10, **10**, **11**

dieffenbachia, *see* dumb cane
dumb cane (*Dieffenbachia*), 25-26, **27**
elephant ear (*Caladium*), 26, **27**
English ivy (*Hedera helix*), **19**, 20-21, **20**
Euphorbia, 10, **11**, 12, 28, 30
four-o'clock (*Mirabilis jalapa*), 10, **10**, **11**
foxglove (*Digitalis*), 13, **15**
  purple (*Digitalis purpurea*), 13
hellebore, black, *see* Christmas rose
hyacinth (*Hyacinthus orientalis*), 6, **7**
hydrangea, *see* common hydrangea
insane root, *see* black henbane
ivy, *see* English ivy
Jerusalem cherry (*Solanum pseudocapsicum*), **29**, 30
jonquil (*Narcissus*), 6
larkspur, *see* delphinium
lily-of-the-valley (*Convallaria majalis*), **7**, 8, **8**
locoweed (*Astragalus*), 23
lupine (*Lupinus*), 23
marvel-of-Peru, *see* four-o'clock
meadow saffron, *see* autumn crocus
narcissus (*Narcissus*), 6, **7**, 8, **8**, 30
nightshade family (*Solanaceae*), 14, 22, 23, 30
oleander (*Nerium oleander*), **29**, 30-31
pea family (*Leguminosae*), 23
philodendron (*Philodendron*), 25, 26, **27**
poinsettia (*Euphorbia pulcherrima*), 28, **28**, **29**

poison tobacco, *see* black henbane
poppy
  celandine (*Chelidonium majus*), 12
  Iceland (*Papaver nudicaule*), 12
  opium (*Papaver somniferum*), 12, **12**
  oriental (*Papaver orientale*), 12
  rock (*Chelidonium majus*), 12
potato (*Solanum tuberosum*), 22-23, **22**
precatory bean, *see* rosary pea
privet, *see* common privet
rhubarb (*Rheum rhabarbarum*), 24
  chard, *see* Swiss chard
rosary pea (*Abrus precatorius*), 23, **23**
scarlet runner bean (*Phaseolus coccineus*), 23-24
snowdrop (*Galanthus nivalis*), 6, **7**
snow-on-the-mountain (*Euphorbia marginata*), **11**, 12, 28
spurge, *see* Euphorbia
star-of-Bethlehem (*Ornithagalum umbellatum*), **7**, 8
stinking nightshade, *see* black henbane
sweet pea (*Lathyrus*), 23
Swiss chard (*Beta vulgaris cicla*), 24
tomato (*Lycopersicon esculentum*), 23, 30
wisteria (*Wisteria floribunda* and *sinensis*), **19**, 21, **21**, 23
yew (*Taxus*), 18, **18**, **19**